Dedication

~•~

Dedicated to Yvonne Gee (1929-2011)
and Harry, both hugely inspirational in their own way.

Copyright

49 Ways To Kick-Start Your Business
Allegra Gee
© 2011 Allegra Gee

ISBN: 978-1-4710-1379-9

All rights reserved. No part of this book may be reproduced in any form or by any means, electronic or mechanical, including photocopying, recording, or by an information storage and retrieval system, without permission in writing from the author.

This edition 2012

Contents

~•~

Foreword 7

About the Author 9

Introduction 11

Getting From A To B: The First Seven Steps 13

Seven Ways To Stay Motivated 17

Seven Creative Thinking Tips 23

Seven Ways To Dance With Resistance 29

Seven New Ways To Think About Fear 35

Seven Social Networking Tips for Business 41

Seven Invaluable Resources When Starting A Business ... 47

Books worth a look 55

Foreword

Allegra has never forgotten what it was like to be an open and creative child. In her book, she has done a fabulous job of reminding us to bring that aliveness and spirit to our work and business. Your work can be your play, and you can get paid for it, and Allegra shows you how you can begin.

Nick Williams
Author of *The Work We Were Born To Do*
Co-founder of www.inspired-entrepreneur.com

About the Author

~•~

Allegra's first toe dip into the world of business was organising a bring and buy sale for Blue Peter which raised £137. Inspired by her success, she started a magazine at school, with Beth Miller, called FAKPOV (From A Kids Point Of View). They published at least three issues.

From these dizzy heights of entrepreneurship, Allegra got a few proper jobs, studied a bit, then a bit more. Got some more jobs, trained as an NLP Master Practitioner, worked as a life coach, got a couple more jobs and then returned once again to her entrepreneurial roots.

During this time she remembered how to play, wrote this book and decided to encourage others how to play.

She currently lives with Harry, three chameleons and a porcupine named Janine.

She can be found way too much on Twitter.

For more information and to learn about playing your way to business success go to www.allegragee.com

Introduction

Welcome to *49 Ways To Kick-Start Your Business*.

This book started as a single tip sheet on motivation and evolved into this small (in size) book.

This is a business book more about you than your business. It's about attitude, focus and action. There are numerous resources with specific practical business information, however if you don't have the right attitude it doesn't matter how much knowledge you have.

The tips are all from my own experience, from books I've read and people I've had the privilege of chatting with.

You may read this book from cover to cover or dip in and out as necessary. However you read it, please enjoy.

Thanks to: Suzie, Glenn and Julie for their comments, Nick W for his contribution and timely insights, Rob and Peter for providing my second home at Flirt Cafe Bar. A special mention to my twitter mates for their huge support, especially #teaminspire.

Illustrations by Deano Pickering

~• Room for your notes, thoughts and inspiration •~

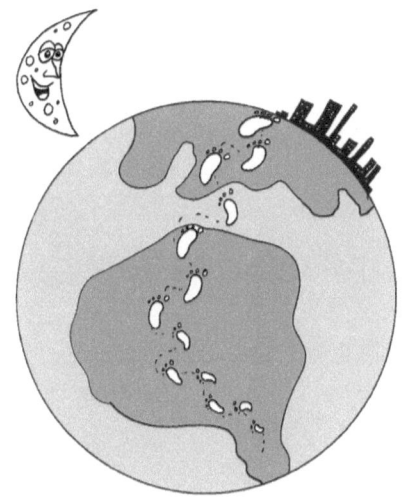

Getting From A To B: The First Seven Steps

~•~

01 ~ Where is A?

Look at your situation now. Start by accepting where you are now. Then look at what you can use from now to help you move towards B.

02 ~ Where is B

What are you aiming for? State it in the present as if it is already happening. State it in the positive, saying what it will give you. Be specific with the detail so you are clear where you are heading. For example, instead of saying "I want to stop working for someone else." Say, "I work for myself".

~• Room for your notes, thoughts and inspiration •~

03 ~ What resources do you need?

To start on this adventure, what do you need? Think of practical, emotional and physical resources and include people. If you were explaining to someone else how they would start, what would you tell them?

04 ~ What resources do you have now?

Of this list, what do you have now? Anything you don't have – do you know someone who does? If it is vital for starting (be aware of resistance) what can you do to get it?

05 ~ Baby steps

Choose your first milestone. It can be as simple as registering your domain name or making your first prototype. All adventures start with a single step. Then choose the next two steps, and so on. Take your time. Take it steady.

06 ~ How will you know when you're on track?

What feedback will you get when you are on track? Once you know what the first step is, how can you track how you are doing? It may be as simple as having a domain name, or a receipt for a venue booked or having a meeting with a client. What will you see, hear and feel? As well as practical feedback, personal feedback is important.

07 ~ Your support network

Who is in your support network? Who wants you to succeed? Think of family, friends, networking people, online support, mentor, coach. Do you need any specific skilled support, such as bookkeeping, administration or web design? (See invaluable resources chapter.) If you have people around you who do not support you, either limit the time you spend with them (if possible) or don't discuss your business with them. Also, remember all the support you do have.

~• Room for your notes, thoughts and inspiration •~

Seven Ways To Stay Motivated

~•~

01 ~ Define your goal

State your goal in the positive and in the present tense as if you are already living it. Keep it simple yet specific.

02 ~ Future pace

Sit with your goal. Experiencing it through the senses can make it seem real. Take 5 minutes to sit in a quiet place and imagine how it will be when you are living your dream. See, hear, feel how it is. You can always come back to this if there are times when your dream is feeling far away.

~• Room for your notes, thoughts and inspiration •~

03 ~ Environment

Where do you work? Are you surrounded by distractions, such as people, noise, and things to do? It is not always possible to have a separate office or space; however it is possible to work with the minimum of distractions. If you do work from home, find a quiet corner. Try and work at the same time each day if you can. Respect your time to work on your dream. You may be able to take yourself out to work. For example, to a café. Most have wifi and can be relatively quiet during the day.

04 ~ Be inspired by those around you

Read a book or article, talk to or listen to inspiring people. It can be a simple quote or a sentence that ignites the spark inside you. It is vital to continue to be inspired. Inspire yourself. Step back regularly. Look at yourself. See yourself. Remember all that you've achieved - however small it may seem. You have inspired many people you may not even be aware of. Continuing on this path of authenticity will inspire so many people. Don't take that away from them.

05 ~ Do something every day...

...towards your goal, even if it's as simple as a phone call, or writing one paragraph. Remember to congratulate yourself. The action of doing something everyday keeps the momentum alive.

06 ~ Who are you talking to?

Stay mindful of who you are talking to about your plans. There are many people who will not support you for many reasons. They may be scared for you; they may be reminded that they are not following their dream. Join or set up a networking group full of people on your side, supporting you all the way.

~• Room for your notes, thoughts and inspiration •~

07 ~ Big chunk, small chunk.

If you are no longer inspired by your dream, and it seems too small, it can help to look beyond it. Ask yourself, what will that give me? Look at the goal beyond the goal. This relights the fire of motivation. Conversely, it can often seem overwhelming, especially at the beginning of a project with so much information and so much to learn. A great tip is to break the goal into small steps and focus on one step at a time.

~• *Room for your notes, thoughts and inspiration* •~

Seven Creative Thinking Tips

~•~

01 ~ No filters

When you are thinking of ideas, allow everything. Don't filter anything. Don't judge any idea. Often ideas can grow on you, or they can lead to other things.

02 ~ Step back

Take an objective look at your idea. Look at it as if someone else were involved. How does it look from the outside? What works, what doesn't work? What would improve the idea? Try to be as objective as possible. When we are not emotionally involved or attached, it is easier to really see things.

~• Room for your notes, thoughts and inspiration •~

03 ~ Environment

Where are you most creative? At home, in the garden, on the beach, on the bus? I work best in cafes. Whenever I sit down with tea, everything flows. It still amazes me how well I work in the café environment. I can work in other places, however it is slightly harder to get going. But in a café, everything flows for me. Try out different places that you can use regularly. It may be a specific room at home, or somewhere away from your usual environment.

04 ~ Be open

Be open to your inspiration. Allow it in. I remember a story I heard once from Jack Kornfield, a Buddhist teacher (www.jackkornfield.org), when he was talking about how he gets inspiration from writing. He sat down to write one day, and someone was making a lot of noise nearby and he couldn't concentrate. He was getting quite agitated and decided to move to a quiet place. Once he sat down in the quiet place, he was able to write. He noticed that he needed to be quiet to hear what he was supposed to write. For inspiration to come to him, he needed to be able to listen. He told this to a number of other teachers who all related similar stories although some needed to see, some listen, some feel. The common thread was being open and available to inspiration. He ended the story by saying that there wasn't an original thought in the room!

05 ~ Intuition

Trust yourself. You have all the ideas and answers inside. Listen to your intuition, your gut feeling. To get in touch with your intuition give yourself some space and some quiet time and ask to hear, see or feel the answer.

~• Room for your notes, thoughts and inspiration •~

06 ~ Morning pages

Julia Cameron (www.juliacameronlive.com) author of 'The Artist's Way' advocates morning pages to help with creativity. It is a technique I have used to great effect. The idea is the first thing you do when you wake is to write three pages of longhand - whatever comes out of your pen. No editing. You don't even need to read it back. It is a brilliant way of clearing...

07 ~ Everything started as someone's idea

When you look around the room you are in as you read this, remember everything you look at was once someone's idea. The difference between what they did after they had the idea and most people, is they took action. They turned their idea into something concrete. You can do it. Think how empty the room would be if those people had just had the ideas and done nothing about it.

~• Room for your notes, thoughts and inspiration •~

Seven Ways To Dance With Resistance

~•~

Inspired by both Nick Williams' writings on resistance and my daily dance with resistance.

01 ~ *Procrastination*

Too busy, too tired, too many commitments, will do it next Thursday – everything will be calmer by then. Need to clean, need to eat, need to sleep, need to see Britain's Got Talent final. Need to buy shoes. Oh look… there's my comfort zone.

02 ~ *I'm not good enough*

It seems from an early age, we are encouraged to compete. And with that comes the almost constant comparisons with other people. Often, instead of being inspired by others doing what

~• Room for your notes, thoughts and inspiration •~

we do, we find ourselves giving up as we could "never be as good as they are". If people have more experience than you, learn from them, don't run away. In the same way, you can share your experience with others with less experience than you.

03 ~ Who am I to..?

Resistance tends to show up when we are on the right track. One of the ways you can tell you are on track is the abundance of doubt and lack of self belief. Even if hundreds of others are doing what you want to do, not one of them will be able to do it in the way you do. So in answer to the question 'who am I to..?' you are you, perfect in every way and with an ability and talent no one can match because they are not you.

04 ~ I'm not ready

One type of resistance Nick Williams discusses is that of perpetual student. 'I can't start until I have done this training or this workshop or finished this book.' There are so many places and ways to study. However if you find you are using the learning opportunities as a way to not do what you are here to do, maybe this is your resistance. The best learning is by doing. Until you start, how can you learn? Theory is hugely important, however practice is where it's at.

05 ~ What if...

The Dalai Lama says that if you are worrying about something and you can do something about it, then do it. If you can't do anything about it, then stop worrying. Resistance breeds in the arena of 'what if...' and 'what if' cannot survive in the present moment. Resistance hates action. So if you feel the 'what ifs' winning, just do something towards your goal. When you are showing up and working, resistance cannot be. Also change the end of the 'what if' sentence. So, from "what if I fail and look stupid" to "What if I succeed beyond my wildest dreams". You never know...

~• *Room for your notes, thoughts and inspiration* •~

06 ~ I'll never earn a living doing that

I read recently about a boy who got a job as a Ben 10 toy tester. There are jobs at Marks and Spencers tasting food. Someone has to check the quality of Thorntons' chocolates…

If you are here to do a job or business and have a passion, you can earn a living doing it. It may take time and it may be in a way you hadn't thought of. There are countless examples of people earning a living doing what they love. There is always a way…

07 ~ How?

We often feel we need to know how we are going to do something, and until we are sure how, we do nothing. This is another form of resistance. Sometimes we know the next few steps, sometimes just one step. The key is to start anyway, because you will know how when you commit and start doing something.

> *"As they act courageously, inspired entrepreneurs make their visions come true but they only learn how retrospectively."*
> **Nick Williams**

~• Room for your notes, thoughts and inspiration •~

Seven New Ways To Think About Fear

~•~

01 ~ Present moment

Jack Kornfield talks about how fear cannot exist in the present moment. We are scared of what might happen, not what is happening. He gives the example of being chased by a bear! He says, if you are being chased by a bear, you are not scared of being chased (what is happening in the present moment), you are scared of what may happen if the bear catches you (the future). He goes on to say how if the bear catches you, you are not scared because the bear has caught you but because of what the bear is going to do next. And so on. His point is that in the present moment there is no fear, as fear is always about what might happen.

~• *Room for your notes, thoughts and inspiration* •~

02 ~ A way for courage to exist

How can you be courageous if you have nothing to fear?

03 ~ How do you feel when you face your fear?

It is very easy, when feeling fear, to stop or run away. Your comfort zone is exactly what it says on the tin. Think back to a time when you faced your fear, however small or big. How did you feel? Did you take the time to acknowledge what you did?

The physical sensations of fear are often the same as the physical sensations of excitement. Maybe it's a question of mindset...

04 ~ Successful people face and go through their fears

It is unlikely that successful people have no fear or that they've just had an easy ride. They do have fears to face, however they look their fears in the eye and carry on regardless. Time and time again. They have the courage to be stronger than their fears. Do you?

"The difference between successful people and those less successful, is that successful people keep moving ahead even when the voice of self-doubt chides them to stop or go back."
Alan Cohen

05 ~ Name it, chat to it, and work out whose voice it is

Accept it and move on. How does fear show itself to you? Is it a feeling? A voice in your head? Next time you feel fear – notice where it is and what it is. If it's physical, stop, breathe three times and see if you can move the feeling from where it is in your body, to out of your body. Imagine moving the feeling. Name it as fear, say hi, accept it and then carry on regardless. It will shrink, if

~• Room for your notes, thoughts and inspiration •~

not disappear with no attention. If it's a voice, is it your voice or someone else's? Turn the volume down on the voice. Or speed it up until it sounds like Mickey Mouse. Is that still scary?

06 ~ *It is your mind that creates this world*

You can play with fear, as seen above. You have a choice. You can feel scared and stop or run away. Or you can feel scared and carry on. There is always a choice of how to react to fear. You can allow fear to win, to stop you and to make you play small. Or you can walk straight through it and carry on (with a sense of achievement).

07 ~ *Fear means you are growing and stepping to the edge of your comfort zone*

This is good. We spend so much of our lives within our comfort zone. Even if it is not the best for us. If we are used to feeling a certain way, the pull of that seems to be so much stronger than stepping out of it. Hence the name...

~• Room for your notes, thoughts and inspiration •~

Seven Social Networking Tips for Business

~•~

01 ~ *Is how we do business changing?*

Have the sell, sell, sell days gone? Is the ruthlessness of the traditional business model history? Maybe. What I love about social networking for business is that it is about building relationships. It is about community and helping each other. It works by building relationships first, helping people and then, down the line, getting some business from that.

02 ~ *Where are your clients?*

Which social networking sites should you use for your business? Which ones will bring you the business? If your clients only use LinkedIn then spending all of your time on Twitter is not productive. So find out where your clients are. You need to think differently to how you think for your social life.

~• *Room for your notes, thoughts and inspiration* •~

03 ~ Turn up and join in.

As Mark Shaw (@markshaw) says in 'Twitter Your Business', you wouldn't set up a shop and have opening hours of 9 – 9.30am on Wednesdays. With social networking for business you need to turn up. Twitter especially is fast and busy, so if you only turn up once a week, no one will know you are there. Invest some time to turn up every day. Contribute, join in with others. Don't just sell or broadcast to your followers, or you will lose them.

04 ~ Your expertise.

Social networking is an amazing opportunity to share your expertise. And it's free. So how might you do this? Build your social networking profile by offering daily tips. On Twitter search under your expertise and join in with any conversations. I know of a number of people who offer surgeries on Twitter. For example, Alan Stevens (@mediacoach) sometimes offers PR surgeries on Twitter, where he offers to answer any questions at a specific time. How can you utilise Twitter, Facebook or other social networking sites in this way?

05 ~ Networks.

As a small business, networks can be a lifeline for support, clients and social interaction. I've made some strong connections through social networking in a short space of time. A good place to start is @purpledognet on Twitter. They promote UK businesses looking to build their business online. In my first month of following them my Twitter network increased 800%! And it's free. There are others doing a similar thing on the different networks, so do some research on any networks you are on.

06 ~ Be personal, be open, be you.

One reason social networking works for me is because I am open and being myself. Some use automated tweets and rarely interact with people. The feedback I've received is that having my photo

~• *Room for your notes, thoughts and inspiration* •~

instead of a logo, and chatting as well as demonstrating my expertise, while supporting others, has kept me followers.

Be yourself, be open, and help where you can. If you employ someone else to do your social networking for you, make sure they are able to interact with your followers, otherwise it won't work. You need to turn up.

07 ~ *Be patient and random.*

Building your online network through social networking can happen relatively quickly, however seeing business return may take time.

For me, being random and connected with anyone (except people just selling) is how I do social networking. From this I have connected with people I would never have come across, all over the world. Initially, I found it difficult to be open and random, however I realised that I was making a judgement based on very little information and how could I possibly know where any connection may lead? I know others who are very specific about who they connect with and that strategy works for them.

There are various ways of using social networking and you will find the way that works best for you. There are numerous social networking sites. Some are open, some are closed, some are just for business. Have a look, try them out, see which suit you for your particular needs. Here are a few to get you started:

- *Twitter* www.twitter.com

- *Facebook* www.facebook.com

- *LinkedIn* www.linkedin.com

- *Ecademy* www.ecademy.com

- *Google+* plus.google.com

~• Room for your notes, thoughts and inspiration •~

Seven Invaluable Resources When Starting A Business

~•~

01 ~ DIY website

A website is increasingly becoming a vital resource when starting a business, even if it is just used as a digital business card. People want to look at everything on the web, and expect things instantly. There are a number of sites that offer basic websites for free or low cost. Some charge for domain names as an extra.

Check out www.moonfruit.com; www.gbbo.co.uk and www.123-reg.co.uk.

If you already have a domain name, you can easily point the domain name to a new site. Some people use a blog as their web page or set up a page on Facebook.

When starting out, think about what you want from your web presence and where your target audience will be. Research what is available and take the plunge....

~• *Room for your notes, thoughts and inspiration* •~

02 ~ The right people

Having the right people around you can make or break a new business. If you are surrounded by people who feel threatened by your potential success or by the fact that you are living your dream it will almost definitely affect you. Many people have given up on their dream when people around them have not supported them. Conversely, surrounding yourself with people who support your dream, can enhance your business.

03 ~ Your team

Think about what skills and resources you have and what you will need. You don't need to do everything on your own, so build your team:

A good accountant won't just file your end of year return they will help you throughout the year with advice. Even if you feel you won't need one when you start, how much do you know about the intricacies of tax when it changes all the time?

Do you need to produce marketing materials, or similar? If so, you may need a designer, and/or copy writer.

If you are writing, do you need an editor?

Having regular contact with a coach or mentor enables you to have support from someone who is objective, someone whose life won't be affected by what you do. However supportive friends and family are it is difficult for them to be completely objective, as it may impact on their life in some way.

It is possible to do all the above without help, however if it is not your expertise then use someone whose expertise it is.

04 ~ Keep things separate

Having a separate business bank account makes things simpler and sends out the right message. There are various business start up deals available.

~• Room for your notes, thoughts and inspiration •~

It is worth thinking about having a separate phone line for your business. Some people will never phone a business on a mobile number. There are a number of options at different prices, from 0800 numbers to internet phones.

It can make it easier to switch off from your business if you have a separate phone line, and as you know it is your business that is being called, you can be professional at all times and make sure it is you who answers the phone.

05 ~ Local or online network

Networks are vital if you work for yourself, especially if you are working alone and from home. Increasingly, online networks are somewhere to start. Social networking is becoming hugely important for entrepreneurs and an excellent resource. (See Social Networking for Business chapter.) Online connections often lead to face to face meetings. On Twitter they are known as tweet ups.

Research networking groups in your area and see which ones suit what you are looking for.

06 ~ www.inspired-entrepreneur.com

'For any small business owners who want to make a difference by building an authentic business around their passions and talents.'

This site is full of inspiration including outstanding free resources, recordings of talks & workshops, and information on events. There are two rates of membership available with amazing member benefits.

07 ~ Attitude

It's great to have all these things in place, however if you don't have the right attitude...

It's about working on your business, not in it. Having balance between your business and the rest of your life. Work towards it every day to keep the momentum alive. Remember your resistance will constantly appear. That's ok as long as you dance

~• Room for your notes, thoughts and inspiration •~

with it and carry on. You can do this. Be positive and surround yourself with people who support you. Remember how brilliant you are and take that step.

~• Room for your notes, thoughts and inspiration •~

Books worth a look

~•~

I read these while writing:

The Business You Were Born To Create by Nick Williams

Know Me, Like Me, Follow Me: What online social networking means for you and your business by Penny Power with Thomas Power

Twitter Your Business by Mark Shaw

Innovate the Pixar Way by Bill Capodagli and Lynn Jackson

Evil Plans: Escape the Rat Race and Start Doing Something You Love by Hugh MacLeod

Thank you for reading this far (even if you started here to see how it ended!) I hope you will refer back as your business grows from strength to strength. Resistance doesn't go away, however we can learn to recognise it and carry on regardless. I would love to hear about your successes and I welcome any comments about the book.

You will find me on

Email allegra@allegragee.com

Web www.allegragee.com

Twitter http://twitter.com/AllegraGee

~• Room for your notes, thoughts and inspiration •~

www.ingramcontent.com/pod-product-compliance
Lightning Source LLC
Chambersburg PA
CBHW021041180526
45163CB00005B/2222